T0413583

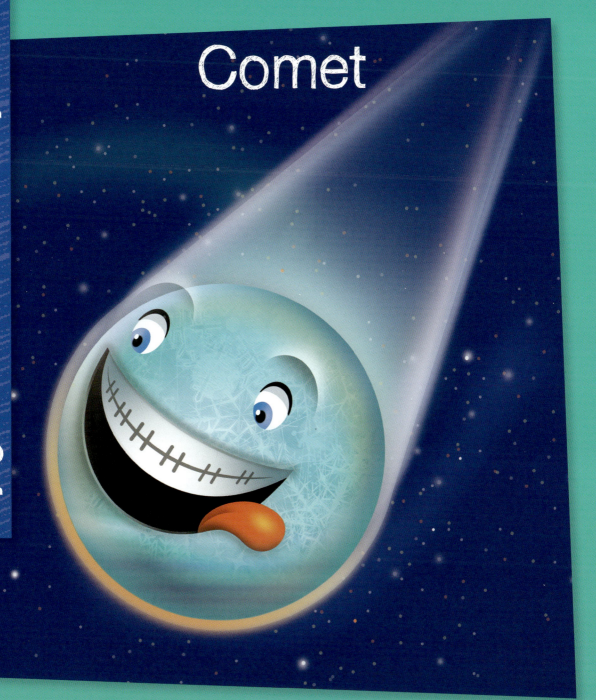

Comet

Cherry Lake Press

Published in the United States of America by Cherry Lake Publishing
Ann Arbor, Michigan
www.cherrylakepublishing.com

Reading Adviser: Beth Walker Gambro, MS, Ed., Reading Consultant, Yorkville, IL
Book Design: Jennifer Wahi
Illustrator: Jeff Bane

Photo Credits: © Triff/Shutterstock.com, 5; © Vadim Sadovski/Shutterstock.com, 7; © muratart/Shutterstock.com, 9, 11, 19; © sololos/iStock.com, 13; © ACD17-0168-009/NASA, 15; © GSFC_20171208/NASA, 17; © Jim Cumming/Shutterstock.com, 21; © solarseven/iStock.com, 23; Cover, 2-3, 12, 18, 22, 24, Jeff Bane

Cherry Lake Press is an imprint of Cherry Lake Publishing Group.

Library of Congress Cataloging-in-Publication Data

Names: Devera, Czeena, author. | Bane, Jeff, 1957- illustrator.
Title: Comet / by Czeena Devera ; illustrated by Jeff Bane.
Description: Ann Arbor, Michigan : Cherry Lake Publishing, [2022] | Series:
   My guide to the solar system | Includes index. | Audience: Grades K-1 |
Identifiers: LCCN 2021036522 (print) | LCCN 2021036523 (ebook) | ISBN
   9781534199002 (hardcover) | ISBN 9781668900147 (paperback) | ISBN
   9781668901588 (pdf) | ISBN 9781668905906 (ebook)
Subjects: LCSH: Comets--Juvenile literature.
Classification: LCC QB721.5 .D48 2023 (print) | LCC QB721.5 (ebook) | DDC
   523.6--dc23
LC record available at https://lccn.loc.gov/2021036522
LC ebook record available at https://lccn.loc.gov/2021036523

Printed in the United States of America
Corporate Graphics

table of contents

About the author: Czeena Devera grew up in the red-hot heat of Arizona surrounded by books. Her childhood bedroom had built-in bookshelves that were always full. She now lives in Michigan with an even bigger library of books.

About the illustrator: Jeff Bane and his two business partners own a studio along the American River in Folsom, California, home of the 1849 Gold Rush. When Jeff's not sketching or illustrating for clients, he's either swimming or kayaking in the river to relax.

I'm a comet. I live in outer space.

I'm about 4.6 billion years old.
This is the same age as the **solar
system**. I was there at the
beginning when it was forming.

I'm made of ice, dust, and rock.

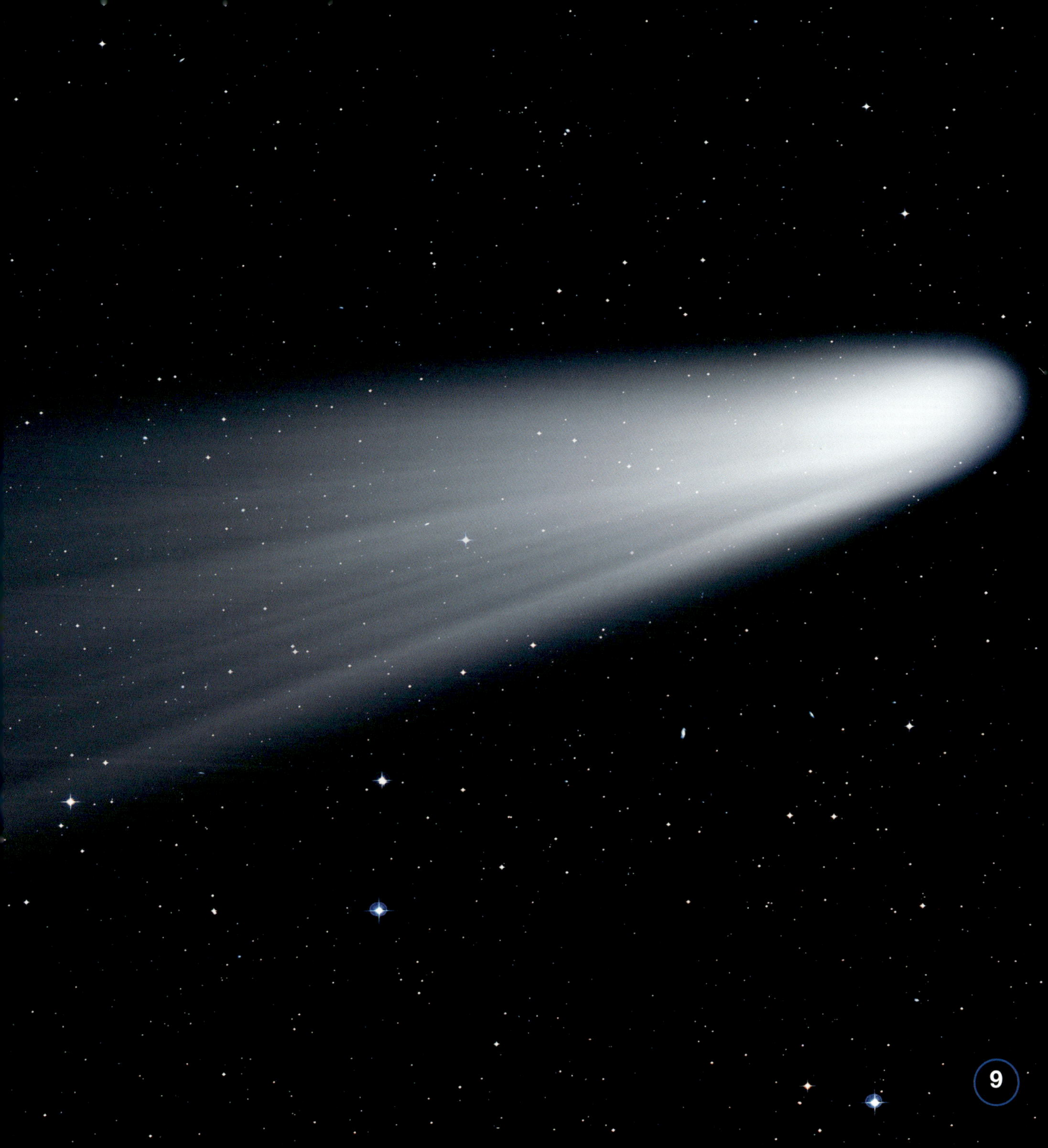

I'm pretty small for something in outer space. I'm usually the size of a small town.

What does your home look like?

There are many of us. We **orbit** the Sun. We live in either the **Kuiper Belt** or the **Oort cloud**.

Short-period comets live in the Kuiper Belt. They have short orbits. Their travel around the Sun is less than 200 years.

Long-period comets live in the Oort cloud. They have long orbits. Their orbit around the Sun can take thousands of years!

Sometimes I travel too close to the Sun. When this happens, I heat up. I form a glowing head and two tails.

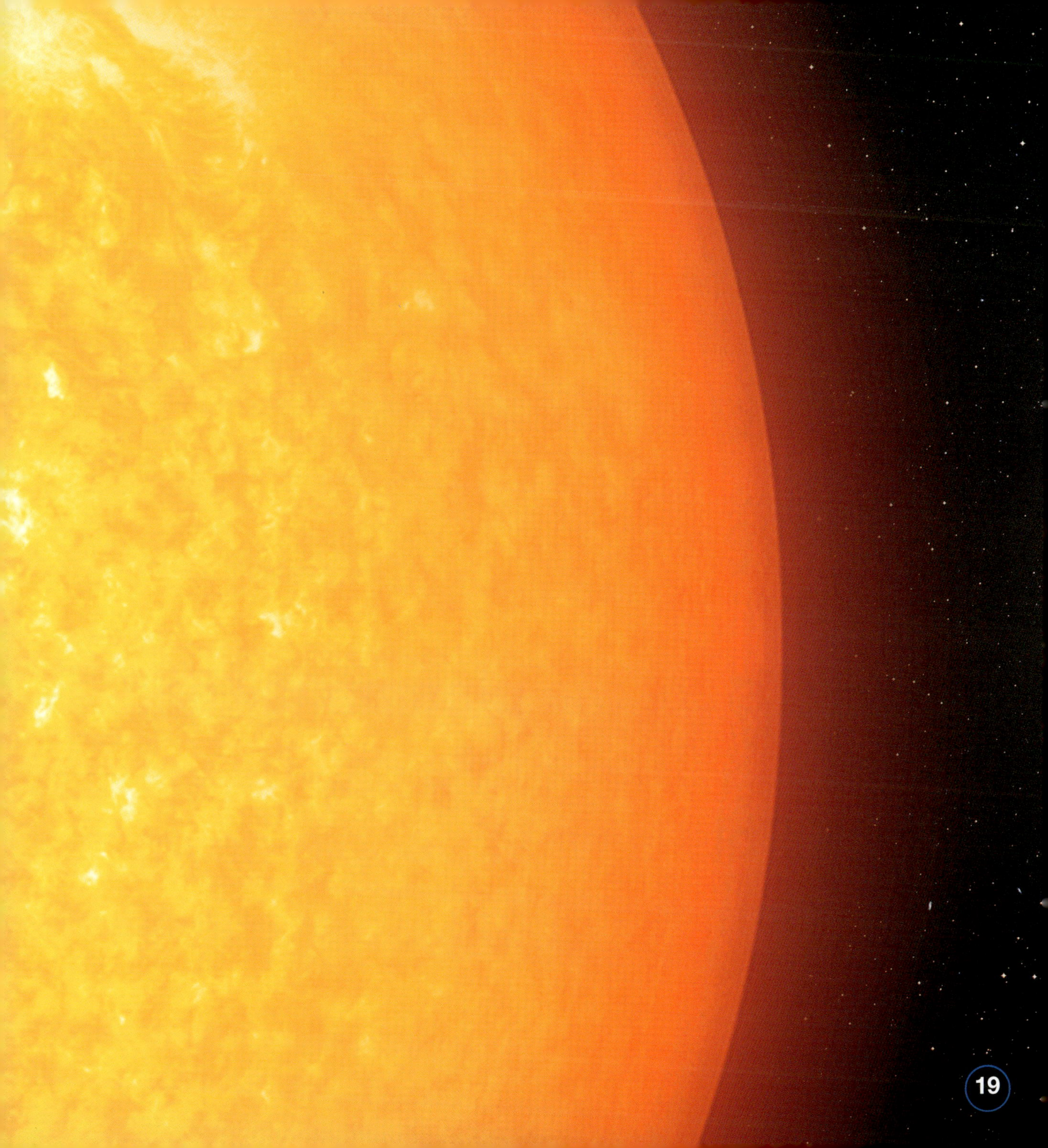

My tails are the **plasma** tail and dust tail. These tails can be very long. This is what people down on Earth see of me.

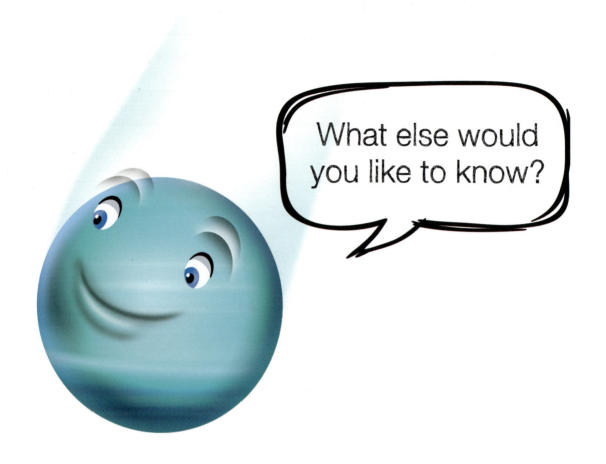

Scientists are still studying me. There's so much more to learn!

glossary

Kuiper Belt (KAI-purr BELT) a ring of icy objects just outside of Neptune's orbit

Oort cloud (ORT KLOWD) a distant shell in our solar system where comets live

orbit (OR-buht) to travel in a curved path around something, such as a planet or star

plasma (PLAZ-muh) a state of matter similar in some ways to a gas

scientists (SYE-uhn-tists) people who study nature and the world we live in

solar system (SOH-luhr SIH-stuhm) a star and the planets that move around it

index